M000083065

TO:

_____

FROM:

_____

DATE:

_____

This is the confidence we have before him:
If we ask anything according to his will, he hears us.
~Isaiah 41:10~

Date: _____

Praises

_____
_____
_____
_____
_____
_____
_____
_____
_____
_____
_____

Confessions

_____
_____
_____
_____
_____
_____
_____
_____
_____
_____
_____
_____

Requests	Answers

Date: _____

Praises

_____
_____
_____
_____
_____
_____
_____
_____
_____
_____
_____
_____

Confessions

_____
_____
_____
_____
_____
_____
_____
_____
_____
_____
_____
_____
_____
_____

Requests

Answers

_____
_____
_____
_____
_____
_____
_____
_____
_____
_____
_____
_____
_____
_____
_____
_____
_____
_____
_____
_____
_____
_____
_____
_____
_____
_____
_____
_____
_____
_____

Date: _____

Praises

_____
_____
_____
_____
_____
_____
_____
_____
_____
_____
_____
_____

Confessions

_____
_____
_____
_____
_____
_____
_____
_____
_____
_____
_____
_____
_____
_____

Requests

Answers

_____
_____
_____
_____
_____
_____
_____
_____
_____
_____
_____
_____
_____
_____
_____
_____
_____
_____
_____
_____
_____
_____
_____
_____
_____
_____
_____
_____

Date: _____

Praises

_____
_____
_____
_____
_____
_____
_____
_____
_____
_____
_____
_____

Confessions

_____
_____
_____
_____
_____
_____
_____
_____
_____
_____
_____
_____
_____
_____

Requests

Answers

Date: _____

Praises

_____
_____
_____
_____
_____
_____
_____
_____
_____
_____
_____
_____

Confessions

_____
_____
_____
_____
_____
_____
_____
_____
_____
_____
_____
_____
_____
_____

Requests | Answers

Date: _____

Praises

_____
_____
_____
_____
_____
_____
_____
_____
_____
_____
_____

Confessions

_____
_____
_____
_____
_____
_____
_____
_____
_____
_____
_____
_____
_____

Requests

Answers

_____
_____
_____
_____
_____
_____
_____
_____
_____
_____
_____
_____
_____
_____
_____
_____
_____
_____
_____
_____
_____
_____
_____
_____
_____
_____
_____
_____
_____

Date: _____

Praises

_____
_____
_____
_____
_____
_____
_____
_____
_____
_____
_____
_____

Confessions

_____
_____
_____
_____
_____
_____
_____
_____
_____
_____
_____
_____
_____

Requests

_____
_____
_____
_____
_____
_____
_____
_____
_____
_____
_____
_____
_____
_____
_____
_____
_____
_____
_____
_____
_____
_____
_____
_____
_____
_____
_____

Answers

Date: _____

Praises

_____

_____

_____

_____

_____

_____

_____

_____

_____

_____

_____

_____

Confessions

_____

_____

_____

_____

_____

_____

_____

_____

_____

_____

_____

_____

_____

Requests

Answers

Date: _____

Praises

_____
_____
_____
_____
_____
_____
_____
_____
_____
_____
_____
_____

Confessions

_____
_____
_____
_____
_____
_____
_____
_____
_____
_____
_____
_____
_____
_____

Requests

_____
_____
_____
_____
_____
_____
_____
_____
_____
_____
_____
_____
_____
_____
_____
_____
_____
_____
_____
_____
_____
_____
_____
_____
_____
_____
_____
_____
_____

Answers

Date: _____

Praises

_____
_____
_____
_____
_____
_____
_____
_____
_____
_____
_____
_____

Confessions

_____
_____
_____
_____
_____
_____
_____
_____
_____
_____
_____
_____
_____
_____

Requests

	Answers

Date: _____

Praises

_____
_____
_____
_____
_____
_____
_____
_____
_____
_____
_____
_____
_____

Confessions

_____
_____
_____
_____
_____
_____
_____
_____
_____
_____
_____
_____
_____
_____

Requests

Answers

_____
_____
_____
_____
_____
_____
_____
_____
_____
_____
_____
_____
_____
_____
_____
_____
_____
_____
_____
_____
_____
_____
_____
_____
_____
_____
_____
_____
_____
_____

Date: _____

Praises

_____
_____
_____
_____
_____
_____
_____
_____
_____
_____
_____
_____

Confessions

_____
_____
_____
_____
_____
_____
_____
_____
_____
_____
_____
_____
_____

Requests	Answers

Date: _____

Praises

_____
_____
_____
_____
_____
_____
_____
_____
_____
_____
_____
_____
_____

Confessions

_____
_____
_____
_____
_____
_____
_____
_____
_____
_____
_____
_____
_____
_____

Requests

Answers

Date: _____

Praises

_____
_____
_____
_____
_____
_____
_____
_____
_____
_____
_____
_____

Confessions

_____
_____
_____
_____
_____
_____
_____
_____
_____
_____
_____
_____
_____
_____

Requests

Answers

_____
_____
_____
_____
_____
_____
_____
_____
_____
_____
_____
_____
_____
_____
_____
_____
_____
_____
_____
_____
_____
_____
_____
_____
_____
_____
_____
_____
_____
_____
_____

Date: _____

Praises

_____
_____
_____
_____
_____
_____
_____
_____
_____
_____
_____
_____
_____

Confessions

_____
_____
_____
_____
_____
_____
_____
_____
_____
_____
_____
_____
_____
_____

Requests

Answers

Date: _____

Praises

_____
_____
_____
_____
_____
_____
_____
_____
_____
_____
_____
_____

Confessions

_____
_____
_____
_____
_____
_____
_____
_____
_____
_____
_____
_____
_____
_____

Requests

Answers

_____
_____
_____
_____
_____
_____
_____
_____
_____
_____
_____
_____
_____
_____
_____
_____
_____
_____
_____
_____
_____
_____
_____
_____
_____
_____
_____
_____

Date: _____

Praises

_____
_____
_____
_____
_____
_____
_____
_____
_____
_____
_____

Confessions

_____
_____
_____
_____
_____
_____
_____
_____
_____
_____
_____
_____
_____
_____

Requests	Answers

Date: _____

Praises

_____
_____
_____
_____
_____
_____
_____
_____
_____
_____
_____
_____

Confessions

_____
_____
_____
_____
_____
_____
_____
_____
_____
_____
_____
_____
_____

Requests	Answers

Date: _____

Praises

_____
_____
_____
_____
_____
_____
_____
_____
_____
_____
_____

Confessions

_____
_____
_____
_____
_____
_____
_____
_____
_____
_____
_____
_____

Requests

Answers

Date: _____

Praises

_____
_____
_____
_____
_____
_____
_____
_____
_____
_____
_____
_____
_____

Confessions

_____
_____
_____
_____
_____
_____
_____
_____
_____
_____
_____
_____
_____
_____

Requests

Answers

Date: _____

Praises

_____
_____
_____
_____
_____
_____
_____
_____
_____
_____
_____
_____

Confessions

_____
_____
_____
_____
_____
_____
_____
_____
_____
_____
_____
_____
_____
_____

Requests

Answers

_____
_____
_____
_____
_____
_____
_____
_____
_____
_____
_____
_____
_____
_____
_____
_____
_____
_____
_____
_____
_____
_____
_____
_____
_____
_____
_____
_____
_____
_____

Date: _____

Praises

_____

_____

_____

_____

_____

_____

_____

_____

_____

_____

_____

_____

Confessions

_____

_____

_____

_____

_____

_____

_____

_____

_____

_____

_____

_____

_____

_____

Requests

Answers

_____
_____
_____
_____
_____
_____
_____
_____
_____
_____
_____
_____
_____
_____
_____
_____
_____
_____
_____
_____
_____
_____
_____
_____
_____
_____
_____

Date: _____

Praises

_____
_____
_____
_____
_____
_____
_____
_____
_____
_____
_____
_____

Confessions

_____
_____
_____
_____
_____
_____
_____
_____
_____
_____
_____
_____
_____
_____

Requests

Answers

Date: _____

Praises

_____
_____
_____
_____
_____
_____
_____
_____
_____
_____
_____
_____
_____

Confessions

_____
_____
_____
_____
_____
_____
_____
_____
_____
_____
_____
_____
_____
_____

Requests

Answers

_____
_____
_____
_____
_____
_____
_____
_____
_____
_____
_____
_____
_____
_____
_____
_____
_____
_____
_____
_____
_____
_____
_____
_____
_____
_____
_____
_____
_____
_____

Date: _____

Praises

_____
_____
_____
_____
_____
_____
_____
_____
_____
_____
_____
_____
_____

Confessions

_____
_____
_____
_____
_____
_____
_____
_____
_____
_____
_____
_____
_____
_____

Requests

Answers

_____
_____
_____
_____
_____
_____
_____
_____
_____
_____
_____
_____
_____
_____
_____
_____
_____
_____
_____
_____
_____
_____
_____
_____
_____
_____
_____

Date: _____

Praises

_____

_____

_____

_____

_____

_____

_____

_____

_____

_____

_____

_____

Confessions

_____

_____

_____

_____

_____

_____

_____

_____

_____

_____

_____

_____

_____

Requests | Answers

_____
_____
_____
_____
_____
_____
_____
_____
_____
_____
_____
_____
_____
_____
_____
_____
_____
_____
_____
_____
_____
_____
_____
_____
_____
_____
_____
_____
_____
_____

Date: _____

Praises

_____
_____
_____
_____
_____
_____
_____
_____
_____
_____
_____
_____

Confessions

_____
_____
_____
_____
_____
_____
_____
_____
_____
_____
_____
_____
_____
_____

Requests

Answers

Date: _____

Praises

_____
_____
_____
_____
_____
_____
_____
_____
_____
_____
_____
_____
_____

Confessions

_____
_____
_____
_____
_____
_____
_____
_____
_____
_____
_____
_____
_____
_____
_____

Requests

Answers

_____
_____
_____
_____
_____
_____
_____
_____
_____
_____
_____
_____
_____
_____
_____
_____
_____
_____
_____
_____
_____
_____
_____
_____
_____
_____
_____
_____
_____
_____

Date: _____

Praises

_____
_____
_____
_____
_____
_____
_____
_____
_____
_____
_____
_____

Confessions

_____
_____
_____
_____
_____
_____
_____
_____
_____
_____
_____
_____
_____
_____

Requests

Answers

Date: _____

Praises

_____
_____
_____
_____
_____
_____
_____
_____
_____
_____
_____
_____

Confessions

_____
_____
_____
_____
_____
_____
_____
_____
_____
_____
_____
_____
_____

Requests

Answers

_____
_____
_____
_____
_____
_____
_____
_____
_____
_____
_____
_____
_____
_____
_____
_____
_____
_____
_____
_____
_____
_____
_____
_____
_____
_____
_____
_____
_____
_____

Date: _____

Praises

_____
_____
_____
_____
_____
_____
_____
_____
_____
_____
_____
_____

Confessions

_____
_____
_____
_____
_____
_____
_____
_____
_____
_____
_____
_____
_____
_____

Requests

Answers

Date: _____

Praises

_____
_____
_____
_____
_____
_____
_____
_____
_____
_____
_____
_____

Confessions

_____
_____
_____
_____
_____
_____
_____
_____
_____
_____
_____
_____
_____
_____

Requests

Answers

_____
_____
_____
_____
_____
_____
_____
_____
_____
_____
_____
_____
_____
_____
_____
_____
_____
_____
_____
_____
_____
_____
_____
_____
_____
_____
_____
_____

Date: _____

Praises

_____
_____
_____
_____
_____
_____
_____
_____
_____
_____
_____
_____

Confessions

_____
_____
_____
_____
_____
_____
_____
_____
_____
_____
_____
_____
_____
_____

Requests

Answers

Date: _____

Praises

_____
_____
_____
_____
_____
_____
_____
_____
_____
_____
_____
_____
_____

Confessions

_____
_____
_____
_____
_____
_____
_____
_____
_____
_____
_____
_____
_____
_____
_____

Requests

Answers

_____
_____
_____
_____
_____
_____
_____
_____
_____
_____
_____
_____
_____
_____
_____
_____
_____
_____
_____
_____
_____
_____
_____
_____
_____
_____
_____
_____
_____
_____
_____

Date: _____

Praises

_____
_____
_____
_____
_____
_____
_____
_____
_____
_____
_____
_____
_____

Confessions

_____
_____
_____
_____
_____
_____
_____
_____
_____
_____
_____
_____
_____
_____

Requests

Answers

_____
_____
_____
_____
_____
_____
_____
_____
_____
_____
_____
_____
_____
_____
_____
_____
_____
_____
_____
_____
_____
_____
_____
_____
_____
_____
_____
_____
_____
_____

Date: _____

Praises

_____
_____
_____
_____
_____
_____
_____
_____
_____
_____
_____
_____

Confessions

_____
_____
_____
_____
_____
_____
_____
_____
_____
_____
_____
_____
_____
_____

Requests	Answers

Date: _____

Praises

_____
_____
_____
_____
_____
_____
_____
_____
_____
_____
_____
_____
_____

Confessions

_____
_____
_____
_____
_____
_____
_____
_____
_____
_____
_____
_____
_____
_____

Requests

Answers

Date: _____

Praises

_____
_____
_____
_____
_____
_____
_____
_____
_____
_____
_____
_____
_____

Confessions

_____
_____
_____
_____
_____
_____
_____
_____
_____
_____
_____
_____
_____

Requests

Answers

Date: _____

Praises

_____
_____
_____
_____
_____
_____
_____
_____
_____
_____
_____
_____

Confessions

_____
_____
_____
_____
_____
_____
_____
_____
_____
_____
_____
_____
_____

Requests

Answers

_____
_____
_____
_____
_____
_____
_____
_____
_____
_____
_____
_____
_____
_____
_____
_____
_____
_____
_____
_____
_____
_____
_____
_____
_____
_____
_____
_____
_____
_____

Date: _____

Praises

_____
_____
_____
_____
_____
_____
_____
_____
_____
_____
_____
_____
_____

Confessions

_____
_____
_____
_____
_____
_____
_____
_____
_____
_____
_____
_____
_____
_____

Requests

Answers

Date: _____

Praises

_____
_____
_____
_____
_____
_____
_____
_____
_____
_____
_____
_____

Confessions

_____
_____
_____
_____
_____
_____
_____
_____
_____
_____
_____
_____
_____
_____

Requests

Answers

Date: _____

Praises

_____
_____
_____
_____
_____
_____
_____
_____
_____
_____
_____
_____

Confessions

_____
_____
_____
_____
_____
_____
_____
_____
_____
_____
_____
_____
_____
_____

Requests

Answers

Date: _____

Praises

_____
_____
_____
_____
_____
_____
_____
_____
_____
_____
_____
_____

Confessions

_____
_____
_____
_____
_____
_____
_____
_____
_____
_____
_____
_____
_____

Requests

Answers

Date: _____

Praises

Prayer is the life blood
of our relationship with God.
Without it there is no communion
+ there is no connection. Of the
essentials of Christian life - prayer
is the most essential.

Confessions

Requests	Answers

Date: _____

Praises

_____
_____
_____
_____
_____
_____
_____
_____
_____
_____
_____
_____

Confessions

_____
_____
_____
_____
_____
_____
_____
_____
_____
_____
_____
_____
_____
_____

Requests	Answers

Date: _____

Praises

_____
_____
_____
_____
_____
_____
_____
_____
_____
_____
_____
_____

Confessions

_____
_____
_____
_____
_____
_____
_____
_____
_____
_____
_____
_____
_____

Requests | Answers